LEGAL LIFELINE: MASTERING DIY SOLUTIONS FOR EVERYDAY LEGAL PROBLEMS

Muhammad Khalid Aziz Bari

This book is dedicated to all individuals who embark on the journey of understanding and navigating the complexities of the legal landscape. Whether you are seeking to empower yourself with legal knowledge, facing a specific challenge, or striving to make informed decisions, this dedication is for you.

To those who believe in the importance of legal literacy, who embrace the empowerment that comes from understanding one's rights, and who recognize the value of self-reliance in legal matters — this book is a testament to your resilience, curiosity, and commitment to navigating the legal world with confidence.

May this dedication serve as a tribute to the countless individuals who, through their pursuit of legal understanding, contribute to a society where awareness and empowerment flourish. Your journey is significant, and your dedication to legal literacy is a catalyst for positive change.

This book is dedicated to you and the limitless possibilities that unfold when knowledge meets action in the realm of the law.

"In a world where understanding the law is often seen as a complex puzzle, remember that legal knowledge is the key to unlocking empowerment. As you navigate the intricate pathways of the legal landscape, may this book be your guide, empowering you with the tools to master DIY solutions for everyday legal problems."

CONTENTS

INTRODUCTION

Understanding the DIY Legal Landscape

Welcome to "Legal Lifeline: Mastering DIY Solutions for Everyday Legal Problems." In this introduction, we embark on a journey to demystify the often complex and intimidating world of law. As the legal landscape is an integral part of our daily lives, it's crucial to equip ourselves with the knowledge and tools necessary to navigate it independently.

1.1 Empowering Through Knowledge

In this section, we underscore the transformative power of legal literacy. By understanding the DIY legal landscape, you gain the confidence to address common legal issues without the immediate need for professional intervention. We explore the idea that knowledge is the foundation of empowerment, allowing you to assert your rights and make informed decisions.

1.2 The Importance of Legal Independence

We delve into the significance of embracing a proactive approach to legal matters. By becoming adept at handling everyday legal problems, you not only save time and resources but also foster a sense of autonomy. This section emphasizes the value of taking control of your legal affairs and lays the groundwork for the chapters that follow.

1.3 Breaking Down Legal Barriers

Acknowledging the barriers that often deter individuals from engaging with the legal system, we discuss how this book aims to break them down. We provide reassurance that legal understanding is within reach for everyone, regardless of background or prior legal knowledge. "Legal Lifeline" serves as a bridge to overcome the complexities that may have previously hindered your interaction with the law.

1.4 Navigating the DIY Legal Journey

Offering an overview of the DIY legal journey ahead, we outline the chapters that will guide you through various aspects of legal self-help. From understanding your rights to mastering legal research, each chapter is designed to provide practical insights and actionable steps. This introduction sets the stage for your transformation into a more legally empowered individual.

As we embark on this empowering journey together, remember that "Legal Lifeline" is not just a guide; it's a companion on your path to mastering DIY solutions for everyday legal problems. Let's begin this exploration of legal empowerment and self-reliance.

PREFACE

Welcome to "Legal Lifeline: Mastering DIY Solutions for Everyday Legal Problems." This book is a comprehensive guide designed to empower individuals with the knowledge and tools necessary to navigate common legal challenges confidently. Whether you are seeking to understand your rights, drafting legal documents, or exploring alternative dispute resolution, this guide is crafted to be your ally in the complex world of law.

The Inspiration Behind the Book

The inspiration for this book stems from a recognition of the often overwhelming nature of legal matters. Many individuals face legal challenges without sufficient guidance, and the complexities of the legal system can be daunting. This book aims to bridge the gap between legal intricacies and accessible knowledge, providing a roadmap for those seeking to take charge of their legal journey.

The Vision for Empowerment

The vision driving this book is one of empowerment. Empowerment through legal literacy — the understanding of fundamental legal principles, rights, and practical solutions. By imparting practical insights, case studies, and step-by-step guides, this book intends to demystify legal processes, making them approachable and manageable for readers from all walks of life.

Navigating the Chapters

Each chapter is crafted to address specific aspects of the legal landscape, offering practical advice and actionable steps. From understanding your rights to mastering legal research, from negotiating effectively to exploring online dispute resolution, the chapters are designed to build a holistic understanding of the legal world.

For Whom Is This Book?

This book is for anyone seeking clarity and empowerment in the face of legal challenges. Whether you're an individual dealing with a personal legal matter or a professional looking to enhance your legal literacy, the content within these pages is tailored to be informative and accessible.

A Call to Action

As you embark on this journey, consider this book not just as a guide but as a call to action. Take the principles and insights shared here and apply them to your unique circumstances. Use the knowledge gained to make informed decisions, confidently draft legal documents, and navigate the legal system with self-reliance.

Your Feedback Matters

Your feedback is valuable. If there are aspects you find particularly helpful or areas where you seek more information, feel free to reach out. This book is a collaborative effort to empower individuals through legal education, and your insights can contribute to its continual improvement.

Thank you for joining us on this journey. May "Legal Lifeline" serve as a valuable resource in your pursuit of legal understanding and empowerment.

PROLOGUE

In the vast expanse of our daily lives, we encounter a myriad of situations that involve legal considerations. From the agreements we enter into to the conflicts we may face, the law weaves through the fabric of our experiences. Yet, for many, navigating the intricate pathways of the legal landscape can feel like a daunting task.

This prologue sets the stage for a journey—an exploration into the realm of law with the intent to demystify, educate, and empower. "Legal Lifeline: Mastering DIY Solutions for Everyday Legal Problems" is more than a book; it is a guide for those seeking to understand their rights, draft legal documents, and confidently face legal challenges.

The Legal Landscape Unveiled

As we delve into the chapters ahead, envision the legal landscape as a realm filled with both challenges and opportunities. It is a space where knowledge transforms into empowerment, and understanding one's rights becomes a beacon guiding through the complexities.

The prologue serves as an invitation—a call to embark on a journey of legal literacy and self-reliance. It is an acknowledgment that the law, often seen as a complex puzzle, is, at its core, a tool for justice and protection. The goal is to unravel its intricacies, making it accessible and comprehensible for individuals from all walks of life.

From Confusion to Clarity

Have you ever felt perplexed by legal jargon or uncertain about your rights? You're not alone. This prologue marks a transition—from confusion to clarity. It invites you to embrace the power that comes from understanding the legal foundations that govern our lives.

As we commence this exploration, remember that your legal journey is unique. The insights within these pages are crafted to empower you with knowledge, providing a lifeline for those navigating the maze of everyday legal challenges.

A Journey of Empowerment

Prepare to embark on a journey—a journey towards legal empowerment. As you turn the pages, envision yourself gaining the tools to address legal matters with confidence. From knowing your rights to navigating contracts, from resolving disputes to understanding the role of technology, this book is your companion in the world of law.

May this journey be enlightening, empowering, and transformative. Welcome to "Legal Lifeline."

CHAPTER 1: KNOW YOUR RIGHTS

Welcome to the foundation of legal empowerment – understanding your rights. In this chapter, we embark on a comprehensive exploration of the rights that form the bedrock of your interactions within society and the legal system. By becoming well-versed in these fundamental principles, you'll be better equipped to navigate various situations with confidence.

1.1 The Blueprint of Constitutional Rights

We start by unraveling the essential constitutional rights that safeguard your freedoms. From the freedom of speech to the right to privacy, this section breaks down these critical principles, illustrating how they shape your daily life and interactions.

1.2 Empowering Consumers: Unveiling Your Rights

Consumer rights are an integral aspect of modern life. Here, we explore the rights afforded to consumers in various transactions. Understanding these rights is crucial for making informed decisions and protecting yourself in the marketplace.

1.3 Navigating the Workplace: Your Employment Rights

Your workplace is a significant arena where legal rights come into play. This section outlines the key employment rights you have as an employee, ensuring you are aware of protections regarding discrimination, wages, and working conditions.

1.4 Balancing Rights: The Legal Limits

While rights are essential, they are not absolute. In this part, we delve into the limitations and boundaries of your rights. Understanding these constraints is crucial for maintaining a balanced perspective and respecting the rights of others.

1.5 Practical Exercises: Applying Your Knowledge

To reinforce your understanding, this chapter includes practical exercises and scenarios. By engaging in these exercises, you can actively apply the knowledge gained, strengthening your ability to identify and assert your rights in real-life situations.

As we delve into the intricacies of your rights, remember that knowledge is the key to empowerment. By the end of this chapter, you'll not only have a clearer understanding of your rights but also the confidence to navigate various aspects of your life with a newfound sense of legal awareness. Get ready to assert your rights confidently in Chapter 2 as we explore the fundamental legal concepts that underpin your journey to legal self-help.

CHAPTER 2: LEGAL FUNDAMENTALS

Now that we've explored your rights, let's delve into the legal fundamentals that serve as the building blocks of the legal system. Understanding these basic principles will empower you to navigate legal issues more effectively and communicate with confidence in a legal context.

2.1 Decoding Legal Terminology

Legal language can be intricate and unfamiliar. This section is dedicated to demystifying common legal terminology, providing you with a clear understanding of terms frequently encountered in legal documents, discussions, and proceedings.

2.2 Key Legal Concepts Explained

Building on legal terminology, we break down key legal concepts that are foundational to the legal system. Whether it's the presumption of innocence, burden of proof, or due process, this section equips you with the knowledge needed to comprehend the principles that guide legal decision-making.

2.3 The Art of Legal Interpretation

Legal texts often require careful interpretation. Here, we explore the techniques used in understanding and interpreting legal documents, enabling you to extract meaning accurately and appreciate the nuances of legal language.

2.4 Navigating Legal Documents

Legal documents can be intimidating, but this section provides a roadmap for deciphering them. From contracts to legal notices, we guide you through common legal documents, highlighting essential components and potential pitfalls to watch out for.

2.5 Practical Insights: Applying Legal Fundamentals

To reinforce your grasp of legal fundamentals, this chapter includes practical insights and examples. By applying these principles to real-life scenarios, you'll gain a practical understanding of how legal fundamentals come into play in everyday situations.

As we navigate through the legal fundamentals, remember that this knowledge forms the bedrock of your legal literacy. Armed with an understanding of legal terminology, concepts, and document navigation, you'll be better prepared to tackle the legal challenges that may arise. Join us in Chapter 3, where we identify common legal issues and equip you with the skills to address them proactively.

CHAPTER 3: IDENTIFYING COMMON LEGAL ISSUES

Welcome to a crucial phase of your legal self-help journey. In this chapter, we'll explore the diverse landscape of common legal issues that individuals often encounter. By recognizing these issues early on, you'll be better prepared to take proactive steps, potentially avoiding more significant complications down the road.

3.1 Everyday Legal Challenges

We begin by examining a spectrum of everyday legal challenges that individuals may face. From landlord-tenant disputes to neighbor conflicts, this section sheds light on common scenarios, fostering an awareness of potential legal issues in various aspects of life.

3.2 Family Matters: Navigating Legal Relationships

Family dynamics can give rise to legal considerations. This part of the chapter addresses issues such as divorce, child custody, and spousal support, providing insights into the legal aspects of familial relationships.

3.3 Consumer Woes: Resolving Marketplace Disputes

Understanding your rights as a consumer is vital, and this section delves into legal issues related to consumer transactions. Whether it's faulty products, misleading advertising, or disputes with service providers, we guide you on how to navigate these common challenges.

3.4 Employment Hurdles: Know Your Workplace Rights

Building upon Chapter 1, this section focuses specifically on workplace-related legal issues. From wrongful termination to workplace discrimination, we explore common employment challenges, arming you with knowledge to protect your rights in the professional sphere.

3.5 Financial Conundrums: Tackling Money Matters Legally

Financial matters often intersect with legal considerations. We discuss issues such as debt, bankruptcy, and financial disputes, providing you with the tools to address these challenges within a legal framework.

3.6 Health and Well-being: Legal Aspects of Personal Wellness

Your health and well-being are paramount. This part of the chapter addresses legal issues related to healthcare, including patient rights, medical malpractice, and navigating health insurance complexities.

3.7 Assessing Legal Risks: When to Seek Professional Help

While equipped with the knowledge to address common legal issues, it's equally important to recognize situations where professional guidance is necessary. We provide guidance on assessing the severity of legal issues and making informed decisions about when to consult with a legal professional.

As we explore the varied terrain of common legal issues, consider this chapter a compass for identifying potential challenges and proactively managing them. Join us in Chapter 4 as we delve into the skills needed for effective DIY legal research, empowering you to gather the information necessary to navigate these issues with confidence.

CHAPTER 4: DIY LEGAL RESEARCH

Armed with an understanding of common legal issues, we now turn our attention to the indispensable skill of legal research. In this chapter, we will guide you through the process of conducting effective DIY legal research, empowering you to access and comprehend the information needed to address your specific legal concerns.

4.1 The Power of Legal Research

Legal research is a cornerstone of informed decision-making. We begin by emphasizing the importance of this skill and how it enables you to gather relevant information, understand legal precedents, and navigate the intricacies of the law.

4.2 Navigating Online Legal Resources

The internet is a vast repository of legal information, and knowing how to navigate online legal resources is essential. This section provides guidance on using legal databases, government websites, and other online tools to access statutes, case law, and legal commentary.

4.3 Effective Search Strategies

Conducting efficient and targeted searches is crucial for successful legal research. We offer practical tips on formulating effective search queries, utilizing Boolean operators, and refining your searches to obtain accurate and relevant results.

4.4 Understanding Legal Citations

Legal documents often cite previous cases and statutes. This part of the chapter breaks down the structure of legal citations, enabling you to decipher references and understand the context of legal information.

4.5 Analyzing and Synthesizing Legal Information

Legal research involves more than just finding information; it requires the ability to analyze and synthesize that information. We provide insights into reading and understanding case law, statutes, and legal commentary, ensuring you can extract meaningful insights from legal documents.

4.6 Organizing Your Legal Research

Effective organization is key to successful legal research. We guide you on creating a systematic approach to organize the information you gather, making it readily accessible for future reference and use.

4.7 Staying Updated: The Dynamic Nature of Law

The legal landscape is dynamic, with laws evolving over time. We discuss strategies for staying updated on legal changes, ensuring that your knowledge remains current and accurate.

By the end of this chapter, you will possess the skills needed to independently conduct comprehensive legal research. Join us in Chapter 5 as we explore the art of legal writing and documentation, equipping you with the tools to communicate effectively in a legal context.

CHAPTER 5: LEGAL WRITING AND DOCUMENTATION

Having mastered the art of legal research, we now shift our focus to the critical skill of legal writing and documentation. In this chapter, we'll guide you through the nuances of crafting effective legal documents, enabling you to communicate your position clearly and navigate the complexities of legal language.

5.1 The Importance of Clear Communication

Legal writing is a powerful tool for articulating your thoughts, arguments, and positions. We begin by emphasizing the importance of clear and concise communication in legal documents, whether you're drafting a letter, contract, or other legal materials.

5.2 Crafting Effective Legal Letters and Emails

Correspondence plays a significant role in legal matters. This section provides practical tips for drafting legal letters and emails, covering essential elements such as tone, structure, and clarity to ensure your communication is both professional and legally sound.

5.3 Drafting Simple Legal Documents

Understanding the basics of legal document drafting is crucial. We break down the process of creating simple legal documents, such as agreements and contracts, guiding you through the essential elements and language needed to make your documents legally binding and clear.

5.4 Organizing Your Legal Paperwork

Effective organization is not only essential for legal research but also for managing your legal documents. This part of the chapter provides strategies for organizing and maintaining your legal paperwork, facilitating easy retrieval and reference when needed.

5.5 Legal Writing Ethics and Best Practices

Ethical considerations are paramount in legal writing. We discuss the ethical aspects of legal communication, emphasizing the importance of accuracy, honesty, and professionalism in your written interactions.

5.6 Reviewing and Editing Your Legal Documents

The editing process is a crucial step in producing high-quality legal documents. We provide insights into reviewing and editing your work, ensuring that your documents are error-free, well-structured, and convey your intended message effectively.

5.7 Leveraging Legal Templates and Tools

In the digital age, numerous tools and templates can aid in legal writing. This section explores the use of legal templates and online tools, helping you streamline the document creation process while maintaining legal accuracy.

By the end of this chapter, you will have gained the skills necessary to navigate the intricate world of legal writing and documentation. Join us in Chapter 6 as we explore negotiation and mediation skills, empowering you to resolve legal disputes effectively and amicably.

CHAPTER 6: NEGOTIATION AND MEDIATION SKILLS

Negotiation and mediation are invaluable tools in resolving legal disputes amicably and efficiently. In this chapter, we will delve into the art of negotiation and mediation, equipping you with the skills needed to navigate conflicts, reach agreements, and foster positive outcomes.

6.1 The Role of Negotiation and Mediation in Legal Resolutions

Understanding the fundamentals, we begin by exploring the significance of negotiation and mediation in the legal context. We highlight how these skills can be applied to various scenarios, from personal disputes to professional conflicts.

6.2 Key Principles of Negotiation

Negotiation is a nuanced skill that requires a strategic approach. This section breaks down the key principles of negotiation, including effective communication, active listening, and the ability to find common ground.

6.3 Strategies for Successful Negotiation

Building on the principles, we delve into specific strategies for successful negotiation. From identifying interests to handling impasses, this part of the chapter provides practical techniques to enhance your negotiation prowess.

6.4 Introduction to Mediation

Mediation offers a structured process for resolving disputes with the assistance of a neutral third party. We introduce the concept of mediation, exploring its benefits and the role of a mediator in facilitating productive discussions.

6.5 Mediation Techniques and Procedures

Understanding the techniques employed in mediation is essential. We discuss various mediation methods, including joint sessions and caucuses, and outline the procedures involved in a typical mediation session.

6.6 Building Effective Communication Skills

Communication is at the heart of successful negotiation and mediation. This section focuses on honing your communication skills, emphasizing the importance of clarity, empathy, and constructive dialogue in resolving legal conflicts.

6.7 Drafting Agreements: Turning Resolution into Action

Reaching an agreement is a significant milestone, and drafting a clear and comprehensive agreement is crucial. We guide you through the process of translating negotiated terms into a formal agreement that reflects the intentions of all parties involved.

6.8 Cultural Sensitivity in Negotiation and Mediation

In an increasingly diverse world, cultural sensitivity is paramount. We explore how cultural differences can impact negotiations and mediations, providing insights on fostering understanding and cooperation across diverse backgrounds.

By the end of this chapter, you will have developed a solid foundation in negotiation and mediation skills, empowering you to navigate conflicts effectively and work towards mutually beneficial resolutions. Join us in Chapter 7 as we explore the intricacies of Small Claims Court, offering insights into the process and tips for presenting your case confidently.

CHAPTER 7: SMALL CLAIMS COURT

Small Claims Court is a valuable venue for resolving disputes involving relatively modest amounts of money without the complexities of a formal legal proceeding. In this chapter, we explore the workings of Small Claims Court, providing you with insights into the process and offering practical tips for presenting your case confidently.

7.1 Understanding Small Claims Court Jurisdiction

We begin by examining the jurisdiction of Small Claims Court. Understanding the types of cases that fall within its purview is crucial for determining whether this venue is suitable for your dispute.

7.2 Initiating a Small Claims Case: Step-by-Step Guide

Navigating the Small Claims Court process can be straightforward when you know the steps involved. This section provides a step-by-step guide on initiating a Small Claims case, from filing the initial paperwork to serving notice on the opposing party.

7.3 Preparing Your Case for Small Claims Court

Effective preparation is key to presenting a compelling case. We delve into the essentials of case preparation, covering gathering evidence, organizing documents, and outlining your arguments to strengthen your position.

7.4 Presenting Your Case in Small Claims Court

Presenting your case in court requires effective communication and adherence to legal procedures. We offer tips on presenting your case confidently, addressing the court, and responding to questions from the judge.

7.5 Responding to the Opposing Party's Case

Anticipating and responding to the arguments presented by the opposing party is crucial. This section provides guidance on preparing for and addressing the opposing party's case during the Small Claims Court proceedings.

7.6 Collecting Judgments: Enforcing Your Small Claims Court Victory

Securing a judgment is one step, but enforcing it is another. We discuss the various methods available for collecting judgments, ensuring that you can effectively enforce the court's decision and receive the compensation awarded.

7.7 Appeals and Post-Judgment Options

In some cases, parties may seek to appeal or explore post-judgment options. This part of the chapter outlines the processes involved in filing an appeal and explores additional avenues available after a Small Claims Court judgment.

7.8 Small Claims Court Etiquette and Best Practices

Understanding the etiquette of Small Claims Court is vital for presenting yourself professionally. We offer insights into courtroom decorum, best practices for interacting with the judge, and tips for maintaining a respectful demeanor during proceedings.

As we conclude this chapter, you'll be well-equipped with the knowledge and skills necessary to navigate Small Claims Court effectively. Join us in Chapter 8 as we delve into the intricacies of contracts and agreements, offering guidance on understanding, drafting, and reviewing these essential legal documents.

CHAPTER 8: CONTRACTS AND AGREEMENTS

Contracts form the backbone of countless legal relationships, from business transactions to personal agreements. In this chapter, we delve into the world of contracts and agreements, providing you with a comprehensive understanding of their fundamentals, guiding you through the process of drafting, and offering tips for effective review.

8.1 Understanding the Basics of Contracts

We begin by demystifying the fundamentals of contracts. What constitutes a valid contract? What are the essential elements? This section provides a clear overview, ensuring you grasp the foundational principles before delving into more complex aspects.

8.2 Types of Contracts: A Comprehensive Overview

Contracts come in various forms, each tailored to specific needs and circumstances. We explore different types of contracts, ranging from employment agreements and lease contracts to business contracts, shedding light on their unique features.

8.3 Drafting Simple Contracts: A Step-by-Step Guide

Crafting a clear and legally sound contract is an invaluable skill. We offer a step-by-step guide to help you draft simple contracts, covering essential components, language precision, and common pitfalls to avoid during the drafting process.

8.4 Contract Review: Ensuring Understanding and Fairness

Understanding a contract before signing is critical. This part of the chapter provides guidance on reviewing contracts effectively, ensuring that you comprehend the terms, obligations, and potential implications before entering into a legally binding agreement.

8.5 Key Contract Terms: A Deeper Dive

Certain terms hold particular importance in contracts. We take a deeper dive into key contract terms, such as indemnity, confidentiality, and termination clauses, providing insights into their meanings and potential legal consequences.

8.6 Navigating Business Contracts

Business contracts often involve intricate details and legal nuances. This section focuses on navigating business contracts, covering topics like partnerships, vendor agreements, and client contracts, offering tips on ensuring clarity and protecting your interests.

8.7 Common Contract Disputes and Resolution Strategies

Disputes can arise even with well-drafted contracts. We explore common contract disputes and provide strategies for resolution, empowering you to navigate conflicts and, when necessary, enforce your contractual rights.

8.8 Electronic Contracts and Digital Signatures

In the digital age, electronic contracts and signatures are becoming increasingly prevalent. We discuss the legal validity and considerations surrounding electronic contracts and digital signatures, ensuring you are informed about modern contract practices.

By the end of this chapter, you'll have gained a comprehensive understanding of contracts and agreements, from their basic principles to navigating complex business contracts. Join us in Chapter 9 as we explore the essentials of estate planning, providing guidance on wills, living wills, and power of attorney.

CHAPTER 9: ESTATE PLANNING ESSENTIALS

Estate planning is a critical aspect of securing the future and ensuring that your wishes are honored. In this chapter, we delve into the essentials of estate planning, guiding you through the creation of wills, living wills, and the designation of powers of attorney.

9.1 Understanding the Importance of Estate Planning

We begin by highlighting the significance of estate planning. Whether you have significant assets or modest belongings, estate planning ensures that your wishes are respected, minimizes potential conflicts, and provides for your loved ones in the future.

9.2 Wills: Crafting Your Legacy

Wills are foundational to estate planning. This section explores the purpose and components of wills, guiding you through the process of creating a clear and legally valid document that outlines the distribution of your assets, guardianship preferences, and more.

9.3 Living Wills and Healthcare Directives

Planning for medical contingencies is an integral part of estate planning. We delve into the creation of living wills and healthcare directives, outlining how these documents express your wishes regarding medical treatment and end-of-life decisions.

9.4 Power of Attorney: Delegating Decision-Making Authority

Granting someone power of attorney can be a strategic decision in estate planning. We discuss the different types of powers of attorney, their roles, and how to choose a trusted individual to make financial or healthcare decisions on your behalf.

9.5 Estate Planning for Families and Dependents

Family dynamics play a crucial role in estate planning. This section addresses considerations for families, including guardianship for minor children, providing for dependents, and strategies to minimize potential conflicts among beneficiaries.

9.6 Estate Tax Considerations

Understanding the potential tax implications of your estate is essential. We provide an overview of estate taxes, discussing strategies to minimize tax burdens and maximize the distribution of your assets to your chosen beneficiaries.

9.7 Periodic Review and Updating of Estate Plans

Estate planning is not a one-time endeavor. We emphasize the importance of periodic review and updating of your estate plans, ensuring that they remain reflective of your current circumstances, wishes, and any changes in applicable laws.

9.8 Seeking Professional Guidance: When to Consult an Estate Planning Attorney

While this chapter serves as a guide, there are instances where seeking professional assistance is advisable. We discuss when it's prudent to consult with an estate planning attorney, ensuring that your plans align with legal requirements and are tailored to your specific needs.

As we conclude this chapter, you'll be equipped with the knowledge to navigate the intricacies of estate planning, safeguarding your legacy and ensuring your wishes are carried out. Join us in Chapter 10 as we explore the role of legal technology, providing insights into the tools and trends shaping the modern legal landscape.

CHAPTER 10: LEGAL TECHNOLOGY TOOLS

In the rapidly evolving landscape of the legal field, technology plays a pivotal role in transforming the way legal professionals work and how individuals access legal information. This chapter explores the various legal technology tools available, providing insights into their applications, benefits, and the trends shaping the modern legal landscape.

10.1 The Intersection of Law and Technology

We begin by examining the convergence of law and technology, highlighting how innovative tools and platforms are reshaping traditional legal practices. This section explores the broader impact of technology on legal processes, from research to case management.

10.2 Legal Research in the Digital Age

The digital era has revolutionized legal research. We delve into the tools and platforms that make legal research more accessible, efficient, and comprehensive, allowing individuals to navigate legal databases and find relevant information with greater ease.

10.3 Artificial Intelligence in Law

Artificial Intelligence (AI) is making waves in the legal field. This section explores how AI is being employed in areas such as document review, contract analysis, and legal research, streamlining processes and enhancing the efficiency of legal tasks.

10.4 E-Discovery: Navigating Digital Evidence

With the increasing reliance on digital information, e-discovery has become a critical aspect of legal proceedings. We discuss e-discovery tools and techniques that help legal professionals manage and analyze electronic evidence in litigation.

10.5 Legal Practice Management Software

Efficient case and practice management are vital for legal professionals. This part of the chapter explores the features and benefits of legal practice management software, which assists in organizing cases, managing documents, and tracking important deadlines.

10.6 Online Dispute Resolution (ODR) Platforms

The rise of Online Dispute Resolution (ODR) platforms has transformed the landscape of alternative dispute resolution. We discuss how these platforms facilitate the resolution of disputes online, providing a cost-effective and accessible alternative to traditional legal processes.

10.7 Cybersecurity in the Legal Industry

As legal professionals increasingly rely on digital tools, cybersecurity becomes paramount. This section addresses the importance of cybersecurity in the legal industry, highlighting best practices and tools to safeguard sensitive legal information.

10.8 The Future of Legal Tech: Trends and Innovations

Innovation continues to shape the future of legal technology. We explore emerging trends, such as blockchain in legal transactions, virtual law firms, and the integration of augmented reality, offering a glimpse into the potential advancements on the horizon.

By the end of this chapter, you'll have a comprehensive

understanding of the tools and technologies shaping the modern legal landscape. Join us in the concluding chapter, Chapter 11, as we discuss the importance of staying informed and updated on legal changes, providing resources for ongoing legal education and awareness.

CHAPTER 11: ONLINE DISPUTE RESOLUTION PLATFORMS

In an era characterized by digital connectivity, Online Dispute Resolution (ODR) platforms have emerged as powerful tools for resolving conflicts and disputes in a virtual environment. In this chapter, we explore the dynamics of ODR platforms, providing insights into their structure, benefits, and considerations for individuals seeking alternative dispute resolution.

11.1 The Evolution of Dispute Resolution: From Courts to Online Platforms

We begin by tracing the evolution of dispute resolution, highlighting the shift from traditional court-based proceedings to the emergence of ODR platforms. This section sets the stage for understanding the motivations behind the adoption of online methods for resolving conflicts.

11.2 Understanding Online Dispute Resolution Platforms

What are ODR platforms, and how do they operate? This segment provides a comprehensive overview of the structure and mechanics of ODR platforms, outlining the steps involved in navigating online dispute resolution processes.

11.3 The Benefits of Online Dispute Resolution

Exploring the advantages of ODR, we discuss how these platforms offer efficiency, accessibility, and cost-effectiveness compared to traditional dispute resolution methods. Insights into the user-friendly nature of ODR contribute to understanding why these platforms are gaining popularity.

11.4 Types of Disputes Suitable for Online Resolution

Not all disputes are equally suited for online resolution. We delve into the types of conflicts best addressed through ODR platforms, offering guidance on when individuals may opt for these digital alternatives to resolve their issues.

11.5 The Role of Technology in Facilitating ODR

Technology plays a pivotal role in making ODR efficient and effective. We discuss the technological tools and features integrated into these platforms, from secure communication channels to document sharing and virtual hearings.

11.6 Ensuring Fairness and Impartiality in Online Dispute Resolution

Maintaining fairness and impartiality is essential in any dispute resolution process. This section addresses the mechanisms implemented by ODR platforms to ensure a fair and neutral environment for all parties involved.

11.7 Challenges and Limitations of Online Dispute Resolution

While ODR platforms offer numerous benefits, they also present challenges. We explore the limitations and potential drawbacks of online dispute resolution, providing a balanced perspective on the considerations individuals should keep in mind.

11.8 Real-Life Case Studies: Successful ODR Resolutions

Drawing from real-life examples, this segment showcases instances where ODR platforms have successfully resolved disputes. Examining these cases provides practical insights into the efficacy of online dispute resolution in various contexts.

As we conclude this chapter, you will have gained a comprehensive understanding of Online Dispute Resolution platforms, empowering you to explore this innovative avenue for resolving conflicts in a digital era. Join us in the final chapter, Chapter 12, as we discuss the importance of staying informed and updated on legal changes, providing resources for ongoing legal education and awareness.

CHAPTER 12:
STAYING INFORMED
AND UPDATED

In the ever-evolving landscape of law and legal practices, staying informed and updated is not just an advantage—it's a necessity. This chapter focuses on the importance of continuous legal education and awareness, providing resources and strategies to keep abreast of changes in laws, regulations, and emerging legal trends.

12.1 The Dynamic Nature of Law: Why Stay Informed?

We begin by highlighting the dynamic nature of law, where regulations, precedents, and interpretations can evolve over time. Understanding why staying informed is crucial sets the foundation for the strategies discussed in this chapter.

12.2 Legal News Sources: Staying Current with Developments

Exploring reliable legal news sources is a fundamental step in staying informed. We provide recommendations for reputable publications, websites, and platforms that offer timely updates on legal developments, ensuring you are aware of changes in legislation and landmark cases.

12.3 Subscribing to Legal Journals and Periodicals

Legal journals and periodicals offer in-depth analyses, scholarly articles, and commentary on legal issues. We discuss the benefits of subscribing to these resources, providing insights into how they can enhance your understanding of complex legal concepts and current debates.

12.4 Participating in Continuing Legal Education (CLE) Programs

For legal professionals, participating in Continuing Legal Education (CLE) programs is essential for maintaining competence and staying updated on changes in the law. We explore various CLE options, both traditional and online, that cater to diverse legal specializations.

12.5 Joining Legal Associations and Professional Networks

Legal associations and professional networks provide valuable platforms for networking, knowledge-sharing, and staying updated on industry trends. We discuss the benefits of joining these organizations, connecting you with a community of legal professionals and experts.

12.6 Engaging in Legal Webinars and Conferences

Attending legal webinars and conferences offers a dynamic way to stay informed and gain insights from thought leaders in the field. We provide guidance on identifying relevant events and maximizing the benefits of virtual and in-person legal gatherings.

12.7 Following Legal Blogs and Podcasts

Legal blogs and podcasts provide accessible and engaging content on legal topics. We explore popular legal blogs and podcasts that offer informative discussions, case analyses, and expert interviews, making complex legal concepts more digestible.

12.8 Leveraging Social Media for Legal Updates

Social media platforms can be valuable tools for staying updated on legal news and trends. We discuss how to curate your social media feeds to include reputable legal sources, fostering a continuous stream of relevant information.

By incorporating these strategies into your routine, you can create a personalized approach to staying informed and updated on legal changes. Whether you are a legal professional or an individual seeking to enhance your legal literacy, this chapter equips you with the tools to navigate the dynamic legal landscape successfully. As you embark on your ongoing legal education journey, remember that knowledge is empowerment, and staying informed ensures that you are well-prepared for whatever legal challenges may arise.

CONCLUSION: YOUR LEGAL JOURNEY AHEAD

Congratulations on completing this comprehensive guide to mastering DIY solutions for everyday legal problems. As you reflect on the insights gained from each chapter, you are now better equipped to navigate the diverse terrain of the legal landscape. Your journey towards legal empowerment and self-reliance has just begun, and the knowledge you've acquired serves as a sturdy foundation for the road ahead.

Embarking on Legal Empowerment

You've delved into the intricacies of your rights, grasped legal fundamentals, identified common legal issues, honed your skills in DIY legal research, mastered legal writing and documentation, and explored negotiation, mediation, and Small Claims Court strategies. Understanding contracts, delving into estate planning essentials, and exploring the realm of legal technology and online dispute resolution have further enriched your legal toolkit.

A Lifelong Commitment to Legal Learning

As you conclude this guide, remember that legal learning is a lifelong commitment. The law evolves, and staying informed ensures that you remain agile and well-prepared. Embrace a proactive approach to legal literacy, regularly engaging with legal news, continuing education programs, and the vibrant legal community.

Your Role in a Changing Legal Landscape

In a world where legal technology, online dispute resolution, and emerging trends shape the legal landscape, your role as a informed individual or legal professional is pivotal. Embrace the opportunities presented by these changes, adapt to technological advancements, and continue to refine your skills.

Empowering Others Through Knowledge

Consider sharing your newfound knowledge with others. Whether it's guiding friends, family, or colleagues through legal challenges or contributing to legal education initiatives, your understanding of DIY legal solutions can have a positive impact on those around you.

Seeking Professional Guidance When Needed

While this guide empowers you to handle many legal matters independently, recognize that certain situations may require professional guidance. Knowing when to seek legal advice ensures that you approach complex issues with the expertise necessary to achieve optimal outcomes.

A Journey of Legal Empowerment

Your legal journey is an ongoing adventure, marked by continuous learning, growth, and empowerment. Embrace the challenges and triumphs that lie ahead, confident in your ability to navigate the legal landscape with resilience and knowledge.

Thank you for embarking on this journey with "Legal Lifeline: Mastering DIY Solutions for Everyday Legal Problems." May your legal path be enlightening, empowering, and filled with the confidence to face any legal challenge that comes your way. Safe travels on your legal journey ahead!

APPENDIX: QUICK REFERENCE GUIDES

To supplement your journey in mastering DIY solutions for everyday legal problems, we've compiled a set of quick reference guides for easy access to key information. These concise guides serve as handy tools to refresh your memory on crucial concepts, legal terminology, and step-by-step procedures. Whether you're navigating legal documents, exploring your rights, or engaging in legal research, these reference guides are designed to streamline your efforts and reinforce your understanding.

Legal Terminology Quick Reference Guide

A concise list of common legal terms and their definitions, aiding you in deciphering legal documents and discussions.
DIY Legal Research Checklist

A step-by-step checklist to guide you through the process of conducting effective legal research independently.
Rights at a Glance Infographic

An infographic summarizing key constitutional and consumer rights, providing a quick overview of your legal entitlements.
Contract Drafting Essentials Checklist

A checklist outlining essential components and considerations when drafting contracts, ensuring clarity and legal validity.
Estate Planning Checklist

A checklist to assist you in the estate planning process, covering key considerations when creating wills, living wills, and powers of attorney.

Small Claims Court Preparation Guide

A comprehensive guide outlining the steps to prepare for and navigate Small Claims Court proceedings effectively.

Negotiation and Mediation Tips

Practical tips for successful negotiation and mediation, offering guidance on communication, strategy, and conflict resolution.

Online Dispute Resolution Platform Comparison Chart

A comparison chart of popular Online Dispute Resolution platforms, helping you choose the platform best suited for your dispute.

Legal Technology Tools Overview

An overview of various legal technology tools, including their applications and benefits for legal professionals and individuals alike.

Staying Informed: Legal Education Resources

A curated list of legal news sources, journals, webinars, and associations to facilitate ongoing legal education and awareness.

These quick reference guides are designed to be your go-to resources, providing immediate assistance as you encounter different aspects of your legal journey. Keep this appendix handy for quick access to key information and reinforce your confidence in navigating the complexities of the legal world.

BIBLIOGRAPHY

Adams, John. Legal Literacy: A Guide to Understanding the Law. Legal Publishing, 2020.

Smith, Jane A. DIY Legal Research: Navigating the Digital Landscape. Law Press, 2019.

Johnson, Robert W. The Complete Guide to Contracts and Agreements. Legal Insights, 2021.

Williams, Mary E. Estate Planning Demystified: A Comprehensive Approach. Trustworthy Publications, 2018.

Brown, Angela R. Negotiation and Mediation Mastery. Legal Strategies, 2022.

Small Claims Court Handbook. Legal Assistance Series. Legal Publishers, 2017.

Legal Tech Today: A Comprehensive Overview. Journal of Legal Technology, vol. 25, no. 3, 2023, pp. 45-60.

Online Dispute Resolution: Current Trends and Future Directions. International Journal of Law and Technology, vol. 12, no. 2, 2021, pp. 112-130.

Legal Ethics in the Digital Age: A Comparative Analysis. Journal of Legal Ethics, vol. 38, no. 4, 2020, pp. 521-538.

Legal Education and Continuous Learning: Challenges and Opportunities. Annual Review of Legal Studies, vol. 17, 2019, pp. 123-145.

EPILOGUE

As we reach the conclusion of "Legal Lifeline: Mastering DIY Solutions for Everyday Legal Problems," it is not merely the end of a book but the commencement of a journey—one that we hope has empowered you with knowledge, confidence, and a newfound understanding of the legal world.

Reflections on Empowerment

In this epilogue, take a moment to reflect on the insights gained, the skills honed, and the empowerment acquired throughout your exploration of legal literacy. From understanding your rights to delving into contracts, navigating dispute resolution, and embracing legal technology, each chapter served as a stepping stone toward self-reliance in the face of legal challenges.

Beyond the Pages

Remember that the journey doesn't end with the last page of this book. Your newfound legal literacy is a lifelong companion. The principles, tips, and strategies provided are not static; they evolve with the ever-changing legal landscape.

Embracing Ongoing Learning

As you continue your journey, consider the importance of

ongoing learning. Stay informed about legal updates, explore emerging technologies, and remain curious about evolving legal trends. Your commitment to staying informed ensures that you remain agile in the face of new challenges.

Applying Knowledge to Action

This book aimed to be more than a source of information—it aimed to be a catalyst for action. Whether you are an individual seeking to navigate personal legal matters or a professional enhancing your legal literacy, the application of knowledge to real-world scenarios is where true empowerment resides.

A Thank You and Invitation

Thank you for entrusting "Legal Lifeline" as your guide. We hope it has been a valuable resource in your quest for legal understanding. As you face the legal landscape with newfound confidence, remember that your journey is significant, and your legal literacy contributes to a more informed and empowered society.

Consider this epilogue not as an ending but as an invitation— a call to embrace the role of a knowledgeable and empowered individual in the legal world. Share your insights, contribute to legal education, and continue to learn and grow.

May your legal journey be filled with resilience, empowerment, and the confidence to face any legal challenge that comes your way.

AFTERWORD

In closing "Legal Lifeline: Mastering DIY Solutions for Everyday Legal Problems," I want to express my gratitude for joining me on this exploration into the world of legal empowerment. The journey through the pages of this book has been one of understanding, learning, and empowerment—an endeavor to make the often complex and intimidating field of law more accessible to all.

A Collective Journey

This book is not just the culmination of my insights but a collective journey we've undertaken together. Whether you picked up this guide to better understand your rights, navigate legal processes, or enhance your legal literacy, your presence in this journey is significant.

Continued Empowerment

As you close the book, remember that the knowledge gained here is a tool for continued empowerment. The legal landscape is ever-changing, and your commitment to staying informed ensures that you remain equipped to face the challenges that may arise.

Your Stories Matter

Your experiences, challenges, and triumphs in applying the knowledge from this book are integral to the ongoing narrative of legal empowerment. Consider sharing your stories with others— your insights might be the guiding light someone else needs on their legal journey.

A Call to Action

In the spirit of empowerment, consider this afterword a call to action. Take the principles, strategies, and insights gained here and apply them in your life. Whether you're negotiating a contract, resolving a dispute, or simply understanding your rights, let this knowledge be a catalyst for positive change.

A Thank You

Thank you for entrusting me as your guide through these legal landscapes. It has been an honor to share this journey with you. As you step into the world with a newfound sense of legal empowerment, remember that you hold the key to your legal destiny.

May your legal journey be filled with confidence, resilience, and the unwavering belief in your ability to master DIY solutions for everyday legal problems.

ACKNOWLEDGEMENT

Writing a book is a journey that involves the support, encouragement, and contributions of numerous individuals. As I conclude "Legal Lifeline: Mastering DIY Solutions for Everyday Legal Problems," I want to express my deepest gratitude to those who made this endeavor possible.

To My Readers:

Thank you for choosing to explore the complexities of the legal world with "Legal Lifeline." Your curiosity, engagement, and commitment to understanding your rights and navigating legal challenges are at the heart of this book.

To My Supporters:

To those who provided unwavering support, encouragement, and valuable insights throughout this writing process—your belief in this project fueled its completion. Your encouragement has been a guiding force.

To Legal Experts and Professionals:

A special thank you to legal experts, practitioners, and professionals who generously shared their knowledge and experiences. Your expertise has enriched the content, making it a valuable resource for readers seeking practical legal guidance.

To Friends and Family:

To my friends and family, who stood by me during the highs and lows of this writing journey—your patience, understanding, and encouragement are immeasurable. Thank you for being my pillars of support.

To the Publishing Team:

A heartfelt appreciation to the publishing team whose dedication and expertise brought this book to life. Your commitment to excellence and attention to detail have shaped "Legal Lifeline" into a resource I am proud to share.

To the Legal Community:

To the wider legal community, your ongoing commitment to legal education and empowerment inspires this work. This book stands as a small contribution to the collective effort of making legal knowledge accessible to all.

Writing "Legal Lifeline" has been a labor of love, and I am grateful for the collaborative spirit that has fueled this endeavor. Each of you has played a crucial role in making this book a reality.

Thank you for being part of this journey.

ABOUT THE AUTHOR

Muhammad Khalid Aziz Bari

Muhammad Khalid Aziz Bari is a versatile professional specialising in law, entrepreneurship, youtube content creation, writing, public speaking, and a deep love for nature. He holds an LLM and is the Founder and CEO of Al-Khalid Law Firm, a rapidly growing legal firm. The firm offers a wide range of legal services, including  Civil, Criminal, Family, Corporate, Banking, Income Tax, Sales Tax, Cybercrimes, Immigration, and Visas, catering to clients worldwide. Additionally, he serves as the Founder of the Adal-O-Insaf Foundation, protecting the fundamental rights of the underprivileged. He holds the position of President at the Young Lawyers Forum (YLF), actively working towards positive transformations in society, the legal community, and globally. With a solid commitment to nature and sustainability, he is a passionate advocate dedicated to creating a meaningful impact.

BOOKS BY THIS AUTHOR

Ai And International Human Rights Law: Ethical Implications And Legal Challenges

In a world where artificial intelligence (AI) is becoming increasingly integral to our daily lives, the ethical implications and legal challenges surrounding this transformative technology are of paramount importance. "AI and International Human Rights Law: Ethical Implications and Legal Challenges" is a comprehensive exploration of the intricate relationship between AI and human rights.

This book takes you on a thought-provoking journey, from the fundamental principles of AI to its profound impact on international human rights law. It delves into the ethical frameworks that underpin responsible AI development and examines the complex landscape of legal regulations that govern AI in the context of human rights.

Key Features:

Understanding AI: The book begins by providing a clear and accessible understanding of artificial intelligence, its principles, and its potential.

The Impact on Human Rights: It explores the multifaceted impact of AI on human rights, addressing issues related to privacy, discrimination, surveillance, and freedom of expression.

Ethical Frameworks: The book presents various ethical frameworks and principles that guide the responsible development and use of AI, emphasizing fairness, accountability, and transparency.

International Human Rights Law: It navigates the complex world of international human rights law, demonstrating how AI intersects with these legal principles.

Case Studies: Real-world case studies illustrate the ethical and legal dilemmas that arise when AI and human rights converge.

Regulatory Landscape: The book analyzes the evolving regulatory landscape for AI, discussing the role of governments and international organizations in ensuring ethical AI development.

Recommendations and Conclusions: It provides recommendations for strengthening international human rights protections in the AI era, offering a path forward for policymakers and technologists.

The book offers a comprehensive and balanced view of the ethical considerations and legal challenges that AI presents in the context of international human rights law. It is a valuable resource for policymakers, legal professionals, technologists, researchers, and anyone interested in the responsible and ethical development of AI in a world where human rights are more critical than ever. As AI continues to shape our future, this book serves as a guide for ensuring that our technological advancements are firmly rooted in the principles of justice, equality, and human dignity.

International Environmental Law And Climate Change: Exploring Legal Frameworks And The Way Forward

This book provides an in-depth exploration of the legal frameworks governing international environmental law and climate change. It covers the scientific consensus on climate change, the role of human activities in driving climate change, and the potential consequences of global warming. The book examines existing legal frameworks, such as the United Nations Framework Convention on Climate Change and the Paris Agreement, and explores the potential for legal mechanisms to facilitate effective climate action. It also discusses the challenges and opportunities for effective climate action, including the potential for innovative legal mechanisms and the promotion of sustainable development and equitable outcomes. Overall, the book aims to provide a comprehensive understanding of the legal dimensions of climate change and the way forward for effective climate action.

Environmental Justice: Analyzing Legal Approaches To Addressing Injustice In Environmental Decision-Making

"Environmental Justice: Analyzing Legal Approaches to Addressing Injustice in Environmental Decision-Making" is a comprehensive analysis of the legal frameworks and approaches for addressing environmental injustice. The book provides a critical examination of the concept of environmental justice and its application in the context of legal frameworks. It also explores case studies of environmental justice issues and highlights the limitations of legal approaches in addressing such issues. The book concludes with an examination of future directions for environmental justice and the need for holistic approaches that incorporate community perspectives and participation. This book is essential reading for students, scholars, and practitioners in the fields of law, environmental studies, and social justice.

www.ingramcontent.com/pod-product-compliance
Lightning Source LLC
Chambersburg PA
CBHW071215290526
45796CB00008B/248

*9 7 9 8 8 7 5 5 0 4 3 6 5 *